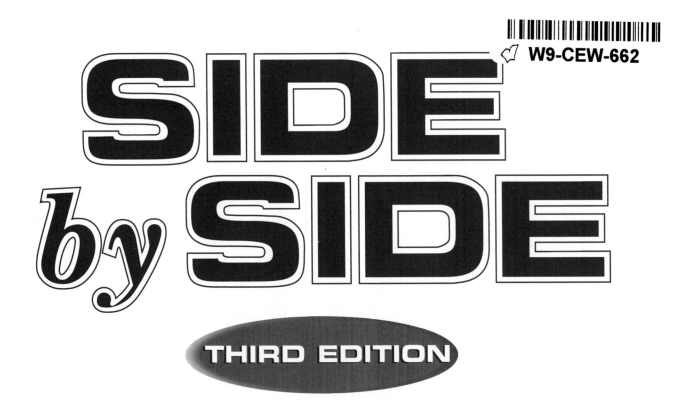

SIDE by SIDE

THIRD EDITION

Testing Program 1

Steven J. Molinsky
Bill Bliss

Contributing Authors

Robert Doherty
with
Donald A. Ranard
Deborah L. Schaffer

Longman
longman.com

Side by Side Testing Program 1, 3rd edition

Pearson Education, 10 Bank Street, White Plains, NY 10606

Vice president, director of publishing: *Allen Ascher*
Editorial manager: *Pam Fishman*
Vice president, director of design and production: *Rhea Banker*
Associate director of electronic production: *Aliza Greenblatt*
Production manager: *Ray Keating*
Director of manufacturing: *Patrice Fraccio*
Associate digital layout manager: *Paula D. Williams*
Interior design: *Paula D. Williams*
Cover design: *Monika Popowitz*

Illustrator: *Richard E. Hill*

The authors gratefully acknowledge the contribution
of Tina Carver in the development of the original
Side by Side program.

ISBN 0-13-026752-X

5 6 7 8 9 10 – TCS – 06

| Student's Name _____ | I.D. Number _____ |
| Course _____ Teacher _____ | Date _____ |

CHOOSE

Example:

_____ your name?

a.) What's
b. I'm

1. _____ your address?

a. Where are
b. What's

2. My license number is _____.

a. (691) 261-3498
b. 26134GB

3. _____ American.

a. I'm
b. My

4. My_____ number is 4-B.

a. social security
b. apartment

5. _____ you from?

a. Where are
b. What's

6. My telephone number is _____.

a. (213) 549-2376
b. 921DGC

7. I'm from _____.

a. American
b. Brooklyn

8. My _____ number is (741) 941-2238.

a. fax
b. apartment

9. My last name is _____.

a. miller@worldnet.com
b. Miller

10. What's your phone _____?

a. number
b. address

11. I'm _____ Florida.

a. to
b. from

12. _____ do you spell that?

a. What's
b. How

13. My _____ name is David.

a. first
b. license

14. I'm _____.

a. my name
b. Susan Lee

15. My e-mail _____ is bob@worldnet.com.

a. address
b. number

WHAT'S THE NUMBER?

Example:

[4]

a. six
b. four
c. five

16. [7]

a. nine
b. seven
c. ten

17. [3]

a. three
b. five
c. ten

18. [8]

a. nine
b. one
c. eight

19. [0]

a. one
b. zero
c. ten

20. [2]

a. three
b. ten
c. two

WHAT'S THE WORD?

Hi	meet	you	I'm	Nice	name

A. Hello. My _____name_____ is Peter Grant.

B. _____ 21 . _____ 22 Susan Lee.

Nice to _____ 23 you.

A. _____ 24 to meet _____ 25 , too.

Score: _____

WHAT IS IT?

Example:

   a. bookshelf
   b. table
  (c.) dictionary
   d. notebook

1. a. pen
     b. pencil
     c. board
     d. book

2. a. computer
     b. wall
     c. globe
     d. clock

3. a. chair
     b. bookshelf
     c. bulletin board
     d. table

4. a. desk
     b. notebook
     c. map
     d. wall

5. a. globe
     b. ruler
     c. book
     d. pen

WHERE ARE THEY?

Example:

A. Where are Betty and George?
B. They're in the _____.

   a. attic
  (b.) living room
   c. basement
   d. dining room

6. A. Where's Jim?
    B. He's in the _____.

   a. post office
   b. supermarket
   c. kitchen
   d. hospital

7. A. Where are Mr. and Mrs. Jones?
    B. They're in the _____.

   a. restaurant
   b. library
   c. movie theater
   d. garage

8. A. Where's Nancy?
    B. She's in the _____.

   a. kitchen
   b. bathroom
   c. bedroom
   d. basement

9. A. Where are you and David?
    B. We're in the _____.

   a. zoo
   b. park
   c. bank
   d. attic

10. A. Where's John?
    B. He's in the _____.

   a. dining room
   b. garage
   c. yard
   d. bathroom

WHERE ARE THEY?

Example:

She's _____ in the kitchen.
- (a.) in
- b. on

11. He's _____ the yard.
- a. in
- b. on

12. The bulletin board is _____ the wall.
- a. in
- b. on

13. The car is _____ the garage.
- a. in
- b. on

14. The monkey is _____ the zoo.
- a. in
- b. on

15. The book is _____ the table.
- a. in
- b. on

CHOOSE

Example:

Mr. _____ Mrs. Grant are in the yard.
- a. are
- (b.) and
- c. am
- d. are

16. _____ John and Jane?
- a. How
- b. Where
- c. Where are
- d. Where's

17. Where are _____?
- a. she
- b. I
- c. Mrs. Lee
- d. you

18. _____ George?
- a. Where's
- b. Where
- c. He
- d. Where are

19. Where _____ you and Tom?
- a. am
- b. we're
- c. are
- d. is

20. Where's the _____?
- a. Mr. Jones
- b. newspaper
- c. Mrs. Sato
- d. everybody

WHAT'S THE WORD?

| He's | It's | We're | You're | She's | They're |

Example:

    A. Where are Bob and Alice?

    B. _ They're _ at the social security office.

21. A. Where's Mr. Lee?

    B. _____ home in bed.

22. A. Where are you and Peter?

    B. _____ in the basement.

23. A. Where's Mrs. Wilson?

    B. _____ at the dentist.

24. A. Where's the cell phone?

    B. _____ in the kitchen.

25. A. Where am I?

    B. _____ in the hospital.

Score: _____

WHAT ARE THEY DOING?

Example:

What's Mr. Green doing?
a. She reading.
b. He's eating.
c. He's reading.
d. She's eating.

1. What's Ms. Wilson doing?
a. I'm teaching.
b. She's teaching.
c. She's studying.
d. I'm studying.

2. What are you doing?
a. We're listening to music.
b. He's singing.
c. I'm sleeping.
d. I'm listening to music.

3. What are they doing?
a. They're sleeping.
b. We're sleeping.
c. They're swimming.
d. I'm sleeping.

4. What's Mrs. Carter doing?
a. He's cooking.
b. She's eating.
c. She's cooking.
d. I'm cooking.

5. What are you and Jane doing?
a. I'm studying.
b. We're studying.
c. We're teaching.
d. I'm reading.

6. What's Mr. Davis doing?
   a. He's listening.
   b. I'm singing.
   c. He's drinking.
   d. He's singing.

7. What are they doing?
   a. They're playing baseball.
   b. They're playing cards.
   c. We're playing baseball.
   d. They're planting.

8. What are you doing?
   a. I'm reading.
   b. I'm eating.
   c. We're eating.
   d. I'm cooking.

9. Where are Mr. and Mrs. Jones?
   a. We're watching TV.
   b. They're playing.
   c. We're reading.
   d. They're watching TV.

10. What's Patty doing?
   a. She's eating.
   b. She's drinking.
   c. She's singing.
   d. I'm drinking.

CHOOSE

Example:

Wendy is _____ in the yard.

a. playing the piano.
(b.) planting flowers
c. watching TV

11. Mr. Johnson is _____ in the living room.

a. sleeping
b. playing baseball
c. swimming

12. Jane is _____ milk.

a. eating
b. singing
c. drinking

13. Karen and Tom are _____ music.

a. planting
b. listening to
c. eating

14. Danny is _____ in the bedroom.

a. swimming
b. cooking dinner
c. studying

15. I'm _____ mathematics in the classroom.

a. teaching
b. watching
c. playing

CHOOSE

Example:

I'm eating _____.

a. a book
(b.) lunch
c. music
d. the newspaper

16. Judy is reading a _____.

a. baseball
b. book
c. guitar
d. bed

17. Mrs. Chen is playing the _____.

a. cafeteria
b. TV
c. lemonade
d. piano

18. The Jones family is eating _____.

a. milk
b. cards
c. dinner
d. the guitar

19. He's cooking _____ in the kitchen.

a. mathematics
b. breakfast
c. TV
d. flowers

20. I'm playing _____ in the yard.

a. baseball
b. mathematics
c. dinner
d. the newspaper

WHAT'S THE WORD?

Where's	are	What	and	What's	doing

Example: Mr. _____**and**_____ Mrs. Clark are playing cards.

21. Jason and Emily _____ watching TV in the basement.

22. _____ are Max and Joe doing?

23. _____ Ms. Johnson doing?

24. _____ your friend?

25. What are you _____?

Score: _____

Student's Name	I.D. Number
Course	Teacher	Date

CHOOSE

Example:

I'm ——— my windows.

a. brushing
b. **washing**
c. feeding
d. listening to

1. She's _____ her hair.

a. watching
b. washing
c. playing
d. painting

2. They're _____ their TV.

a. feeding
b. brushing
c. fixing
d. washing

3. We're _____ our homework.

a. cleaning
b. washing
c. drinking
d. doing

4. I'm _____ my bathroom.

a. swimming
b. planting
c. painting
d. brushing

5. Ms. Grant is _____ her dog.

a. sleeping
b. feeding
c. singing
d. playing

6. I'm brushing my _____.

a. teeth
b. apartment
c. yard
d. wall

7. They're reading their _____.

a. library
b. dinner
c. desk
d. e-mail

8. She's feeding her _____.

a. car
b. cat
c. cards
d. kitchen

9. He's cleaning his _____.

a. homework
b. exercises
c. attic
d. notebook

10. We're washing _____.

a. TV
b. flowers
c. our teeth
d. our car

WHAT'S THE RESPONSE?

Example:

Is Mrs. Clark busy?

a. Yes, he is.
(b.) Yes, she is.
c. He's in the park.
d. Yes. She's Mrs. Clark.

11. Are you busy?

a. You're in the bedroom.
b. Yes, he is.
c. Yes, I am.
d. Yes, they are.

12. What's she doing?

a. Yes, he is.
b. She's cleaning her apartment.
c. Yes, she is.
d. She's doing.

13. Is he busy?

a. Yes, he is.
b. Yes, I am.
c. They're doing their exercises.
d. She's reading her e-mail.

14. What are you doing?

a. Yes, I am.
b. You're at the beach.
c. Yes, you are.
d. I'm fixing my bicycle.

15. Where are they?

a. They're in the kitchen.
b. They're busy.
c. Yes, they are.
d. They busy.

CHOOSE

Example:

_____ she busy?

(a.) Is
b. Are
c. Am

16. _____ painting their living room.

a. They
b. They're
c. Their

17. The dog is eating _____ dinner.

a. it's
b. its
c. it

18. We're cleaning _____ yard.

a. our
b. are
c. we're

19. You're brushing _____ teeth.

a. you're
b. you
c. your

20. _____ fixing his sink.

a. He's
b. His
c. He

WHAT'S THE WORD?

its	our	your	their	her	my

Example: I'm feeding ____my____ dog.

21. We're painting _____ apartment.

22. She's brushing _____ hair.

23. The dog is eating _____ dinner.

24. Mr. and Mrs. Chen are doing _____ exercises.

25. You're fixing _____ car.

Score: _____

CHOOSE

Example:

Is he tall or _____?

a. new
b. short
c. ugly
d. thin

1. Are they rich or _____?

a. poor
b. beautiful
c. single
d. married

2. Is Nancy's cat ugly or _____?

a. quiet
b. heavy
c. pretty
d. loud

3. Is the restaurant expensive or _____?

a. old
b. easy
c. new
d. cheap

4. Is he young or _____?

a. old
b. poor
c. handsome
d. heavy

5. Is their new car quiet or _____?

a. large
b. noisy
c. old
d. cheap

6. Are the questions easy or _____?

a. difficult
b. beautiful
c. fat
d. poor

7. Is their dog thin or _____?

a. little
b. tall
c. new
d. heavy

8. Are you married or _____?

a. handsome
b. single
c. poor
d. new

9. Is your bedroom big or _____?

a. quiet
b. easy
c. small
d. large

10. Is it hot or _____?

a. cold
b. cheap
c. short
d. fat

WHAT THE RESPONSE?

Example:

Tell me about your computer. Is it new?

(a.) No, it isn't.
b. Yes, I am.
c. No. It's small.

11. Tell me about Alice and Tim. Are they married?

a. Yes, we are.
b. Yes, you are.
c. No, they aren't.

12. Tell me about Jack's cat. Is it big?

a. No, it isn't.
b. No, I'm not.
c. Yes, it isn't.

13. Hello. Is this Tom?

a. No, he isn't.
b. Yes, it is.
c. Yes, he is.

14. How are the questions? Are they easy or difficult?

a. Yes, they are.
b. Their difficult.
c. They're easy.

15. Is it sunny today?

a. Yes. It's cloudy.
b. No. It's raining.
c. No. It's hot.

CHOOSE

Example:

It's warm _____ Miami.

(a.) in
b. on
c. to

16. Tell me _____ your neighbors.

a. to
b. about
c. for

17. _____ the weather?

a. How's
b. Where's
c. What

18. I'm _____ in British Colombia.

a. snowing
b. from
c. on vacation

19. Hi, Julie. _____ is Anna.

a. This
b. Hello
c. It's

20. _____ sunny in Los Angeles today.

a. Is it
b. It's
c. Is

WHICH WORD?

Example:

Is the restaurant expensive | and (or) on | cheap?

21. Is | your sister   you're   your sister's | apartment large?

22. | I'm   I'm not   Am I | married. I'm single.

23. Tell me about your neighbors. | Are   Or   Our | they quiet?

24. | You're   Are   Jack's | boss is young.

25. Is | his car new   his new car   new his car | beautiful?

Score: _____

**CHAPTER 6 TEST**

Student's Name	I.D. Number
Course	Teacher	Date

WHO ARE THEY?

Example:

Bob is Susan's _____.

a. brother
b. husband
c. uncle
d. son

1. Susan is Bob's _____.

a. sister
b. mother
c. wife
d. daughter

2. Billy is Patty's _____.

a. son
b. sister
c. father
d. brother

3. Patty is Bob and Susan's _____.

a. son
b. daughter
c. granddaughter
d. niece

4. Bob and Susan are Billy's _____.

a. grandparents
b. children
c. parents
d. brother and sister

5. Billy is Bob and Susan's _____.

a. grandson
b. son
c. cousin
d. nephew

WHO ARE THEY?

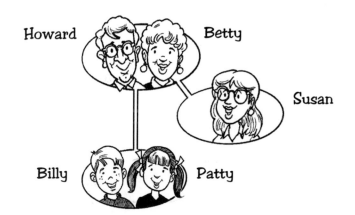

6. Howard is Susan's _____.

    a. grandfather

    b. uncle

    c. father

    d. nephew

7. Betty is Patty's _____.

    a. grandmother

    b. mother

    c. aunt

    d. niece

8. Billy is Howard and Betty's _____.

    a. son

    b. grandson

    c. nephew

    d. granddaughter

9. Howard and Betty are Patty's _____.

    a. parents

    b. aunt and uncle

    c. mother and father

    d. grandparents

10. Billy and Patty are Howard and Betty's _____.

    a. children

    b. son and daughter

    c. grandchildren

    d. cousins

WHAT ARE THEY DOING?

Example:

Mrs. Jackson is _____ in the garden.

a. vacuuming
b. planting flowers
c. fixing flowers

11. Albert is _____ in the living room.

a. sleeping
b. singing
c. making noise

12. Carol is _____.

a. skateboarding
b. playing her bicycle
c. riding her bicycle

13. My friends are —— at my sister's wedding.

a. singing
b. crying
c. laughing

14. Tim is _____ at school.

a. watching a play
b. playing
c. acting in a play

15. Mr. and Mrs. Carter are _____ in the dining room.

a. having dinner
b. looking
c. dancing

WHAT'S THE QUESTION?

Example:

A. _____?
B. My name is Jane.
  ⓐ What's your name?
  b. Where are you?
  c. Who are you?
  d. Who is she?

16. A. _____?
B. They're my cousins.
  a. Who are you?
  b. What are they?
  c. Who are they?
  d. What are they?

17. A. _____?
B. She's playing the drums.
  a. Where's Mrs. Park?
  b. What's Mrs. Park doing?
  c. What's Mr. Park doing?
  d. Where is Mrs. Park playing?

18. A. _____?
B. He's my father.
  a. What's he doing?
  b. Where is he?
  c. What's his name?
  d. Who is he?

19. A. _____?
B. They're in Washington D.C.
  a. Who are they?
  b. Where's your cousin?
  c. Where are they?
  d. What are they doing?

20. A. _____?
B. We're washing our car.
  a. What are they doing?
  b. Where are you?
  c. What am I doing?
  d. What are you doing?

WHICH WORD?

Example:

My grandfather | (is)   in   are | very tired.

21. My aunt is sitting | at   in   on | the sofa.

22. My uncle is having lunch | in   or   on | the kitchen.

23. We're washing our car | on   in   in front of | our house.

24. My friends are singing | at   in   of | my birthday party.

25. This is a photograph | on   or   of | my brother and me.

Score: _____

Student's Name _____	I.D. Number _____
Course _____	Teacher _____	Date _____

WHERE IS IT?

Example:

The restaurant is _____ the bank.

(a.) next to
b. between
c. across from

1. The library is _____ the barber shop.

a. between
b. across from
c. around the corner from

2. The bakery is _____ the video store and the book store.

a. between
b. in front of
c. around the corner from

3. The health club is _____ the department store.

a. next to
b. between
c. around the corner from

4. The _____ is across from the church.

a. fire station
b. movie theater
c. laundromat

5. The _____ is next to the hair salon.

a. train station
b. bus station
c. gas station

CHOOSE

Example:

_____ the supermarket?

a. There
(b.) Where's
c. Where
d. Is

6. There's a park _____ State Street.

a. in
b. in front of
c. between
d. on

7. _____ a clinic on Central Avenue.

a. Is there
b. Is
c. There's
d. There

8. _____ rooms are there in the apartment?

a. How many
b. What are
c. How are
d. Are many

9. There's an _____ in the bedroom.

a. closet
b. clock
c. air conditioner
d. window

10. _____ a laundromat in this neighborhood?

a. Is
b. There
c. Are there
d. Is there

CHOOSE

Example:

There are six apartments in the _____.

a. roof
(b.) building
c. elevator

11. Are there any _____ in the wall?

a. malls
b. people
c. holes

12. There's a _____ in the basement.

a. washing machine
b. bus stop
c. mice

13. There are three _____ in the dining room.

a. floors
b. windows
c. closet

14. Is there a _____ in the kitchen?

a. refrigerator
b. jacuzzi
c. store

15. There's _____ in the living room.

a. a fire escape
b. are holes
c. an air conditioner

CHOOSE

Example:

A. _____ a superintendent in the building?
B. Yes, there is.
   a. Is
   b. There
   c. Is their
   (d.) Is there

16. A. How many floors _____ in the building?
    B. There are five floors.
       a. there are
       b. are there
       c. is there
       d. are their

17. A. Is there a stove in the kitchen?
    B. _____.
       a. No, there is.
       b. Yes, there's.
       c. Yes, there is.
       d. Yes, is there.

18. A. There's a bus stop _____ the building.
    B. Oh, good.
       a. near
       b. in
       c. on
       d. to

19. A. Are there any children in the building?
    B. _____.
       a. Yes, they are.
       b. Yes, are there.
       c. No, there are.
       d. Yes, there are.

20. A. Thank you.
    B. _____.
       a. Your welcome.
       b. You're welcome.
       c. Welcome.
       d. You welcome.

WHAT'S THE WORD?

| cats | closet | elevator | mailbox | satellite dish | windows |

Example: There's a __satellite dish__ on the roof.

21. There's a big _____ in the bedroom.

22. There's a _____ next to the building.

23. There's an _____ in the building.

24. There are two _____ in the dining room

25. There aren't any dogs in the building, but there are two _____.

Score: _____

| Student's Name _____ | I.D. Number _____ |
| Course _____ | Teacher _____ | Date _____ |

CHOOSE

Example:

I'm looking for a _____.

a. mittens
b. pair of mittens
c. umbrella
d. blouses

1. Those _____ are small.

   a. gloves
   b. pair of gloves
   c. glove
   d. dress

2. There's a _____ on the chair.

   a. earring
   b. mitten
   c. watches
   d. pants

3. I'm looking for a _____.

   a. socks
   b. striped
   c. jeans
   d. briefcase

4. Those are very expensive _____.

   a. dress
   b. watches
   c. sock
   d. necklace

5. _____ are over there.

   a. Glasses
   b. Purse
   c. Blouse
   d. Glove

6. _____ this your earring?

   a. Is
   b. Are
   c. His
   d. Here's

7. Purple _____ are very popular this year.

   a. sports jacket
   b. sunglass
   c. pajamas
   d. purse

8. But these are _____!

   a. gloves green
   b. green gloves
   c. green glove
   d. glove green

9. Here's an _____ hat.

   a. very nice
   b. wool
   c. inexpensive
   d. pretty

10. I'm looking for a pair of _____.

    a. dress
    b. blouse
    c. pant
    d. jeans

WHICH WORD DOESN'T BELONG?

Example:

      a. socks   b. stockings   (c.) jeans   d. shoes

11. a. bracelet   b. necklace   c. earrings   d. mittens

12. a. boy   b. belt   c. child   d. person

13. a. raincoat   b. boots   c. sunglasses   d. umbrella

14. a. polka dot   b. pink   c. gold   d. red

15. a. sweater   b. shirt   c. socks   d. sports jacket

CHOOSE

Example:

_____ gloves are very nice.
a. This
(b.) These
c. That

18. I think _____ are my socks.
a. this
b. that
c. those

16. But _____ is a striped hat!
a. these
b. those
c. this

19. _____ blouse is pretty.
a. Those
b. This
c. These

17. Is _____ your tie?
a. that
b. those
c. these

20. Are _____ your pajamas?
a. this
b. that
c. these

WHICH WORD?

A. Excuse me. I think | this   it   (that's) | my bracelet.

B. Hmm. I don't think so. I think | this   these   that's |²¹ is MY bracelet.

A. Oh. | Your   That   You're |²² right. I guess I made a mistake.

A. Can I help you?

B. Yes, please. I'm looking for | pair of   a pair of   a pair |²³ mittens.

A. ' | Here   This is   These are |²⁴ very nice mittens.

B. But | those   are those   those are |²⁵ polka dot mittens!

Score: _____

Student's Name _____ I.D. Number _____

Course _____ Teacher _____ Date _____

CHOOSE

Example:

   A. What's he doing?
   B. He's _____ his rug.
     a. watching
     (b.) vacuuming
     c. painting
     d. looking

1. A. What's your name?
   B. _____ name is Pat.
     a. My
     b. His
     c. Her
     d. Your

2. A. Where are your friends?
   B. _____ are at school.
     a. We
     b. You
     c. They
     d. They're

3. A. What's Bob wearing?
   B. He's wearing a pair _____.
     a. brown of pants
     b. of pants brown
     c. brown pants
     d. of brown pants

4. A. What are you doing?
   B. We're _____.
     a. cook
     b. cooking
     c. our cooking
     d. are cooking

5. A. Is it very warm in Honolulu?
   B. Yes. It's _____.
     a. hot
     b. snowing
     c. cold
     d. cool

6. A. Are you washing your clothes?
   B. No, _____.
     a. I am
     b. I not
     c. I'm not
     d. you are

7. A. Is your VCR old?
   B. No, it isn't. It's _____.
     a. tall
     b. young
     c. quiet
     d. new

8. A. Can I help you?
   B. Yes. I'm looking for a _____.
     a. blouse
     b. gloves
     c. umbrella
     d. dresses

9. A. Is this Ms. Watson's car?
   B. No. _____ car is green.
     a. Her
     b. It's
     c. She
     d. His

10. A. Where's the _____?
    B. It's in the classroom.
       a. attic
       b. shower
       c. globe
       d. school

11. A. What's your son doing?
    B. He's _____ his teeth.
       a. eating
       b. brushing
       c. painting
       d. drinking

12. A. Is this Tom?
    B. Yes, _____.
       a. he is
       b. it is
       c. it's is
       d. I am

13. A. Is Bob's dog thin?
    B. No. It's _____.
       a. heavy
       b. small
       c. tall
       d. short

14. A. _____ are they?
    B. They're in San Francisco.
       a. Who
       b. How
       c. Where's
       d. Where

15. A. Where's the dictionary?
    B. _____ in the living room.
       a. It's
       b. Its
       c. He's
       d. Is

CHOOSE

Example:

They're making a lot _____ noise.
(a.) of
b. a
c. to
d. for

16. The television is _____ front of
    the window.
    a. on
    b. in
    c. at
    d. a

17. _____ is the post office?
    a. Where
    b. What
    c. Who
    d. Where's

18. _____ a school near the park.
    a. These
    b. They
    c. There's
    d. Is

19. My father's sister is my _____.

   a. cousin

   b. daughter

   c. grandmother

   d. aunt

20. Are _____ your pencils?

   a. this

   b. those

   c. that

   d. these are

21. There aren't any _____ in this neighborhood.

   a. book store

   b. clinic

   c. parks

   d. cafeteria

22. Those _____ are large.

   a. houses

   b. house

   c. house's

   d. office

23. She's my _____.

   a. husband

   b. niece

   c. brother

   d. nephew

24. _____ many windows are there in the living room?

   a. Who

   b. What

   c. Are

   d. How

25. My children are doing _____ homework.

   a their

   b. there

   c. these

   d. they're

26. My favorite color is _____.

   a. broken

   b. blue

   c. big

   d. striped

27. Mrs. Chen is _____ in the park.

   a. raining

   b. feeding

   c. reading

   d. fixing

28. Nice to _____ you.

   a. hello

   b. spell

   c. tell

   d. meet

29. There aren't any _____ here.

   a. children

   b. man

   c. child

   d. parent

30. He's swimming _____ the beach.

   a. in

   b. at

   c. for

   d. on

31. Is _____ your necklace?

    a. these

    b. those

    c. this

    d. that's

32. Carol _____ Jim are eating breakfast.

    a. and

    b. at

    c. our

    d. or

33. Is there a TV in _____ bedroom?

    a. are

    b. you're

    c. you

    d. your

34. My mother's brother is my _____.

    a. son

    b. uncle

    c. grandfather

    d. father

35. Where _____ you from?

    a. our

    b. are

    c. is

    d. for

36. My daughter is _____ her homework.

    a. having

    b. playing

    c. doing

    d. calling

37. Joe is studying _____.

    a. dinner

    b. the library

    c. the radio

    d. mathematics

38. _____ me. I'm looking for a belt.

    a. Sorry

    b. Hi

    c. Excuse

    d. Tell

39. What's your _____?

    a. house

    b. address

    c. doing

    d. live

40. _____ a computer in the library?

    a. Is there

    b. Is their

    c. There

    d. Their is

WHICH WORD?

These (This) It's — is my neighborhood. My house is | on in at |[41]

Pine Street. Near my house | they're it there |[42] is a library. My school is around the

corner | from to at |[43] the library. My friend | Jack Jack's Jack is |[44] house

is | across next between |[45] to my house.

It's a beautiful day today. Jack and I | is am are |[46] playing outside in my

| bedroom kitchen yard |[47] . | We're They're You're |[48] playing baseball.

| Our Their My |[49] mother is happy we aren't playing in the house. We're very

| noisy new thin |[50] .

Score: _____

Student's Name _____   I.D. Number _____

Course _____   Teacher _____   Date _____

CHOOSE

Example:

She _____ the piano.

a. play
(b.) plays

1. John _____ a bus.

a. drive
b. drives

2. I _____ American food.

a. cook
b. cooks

3. My sister _____ her bicycle every day.

a. ride
b. rides

4. They _____ French newspapers.

a. read
b. reads

5. My wife and I _____ in London.

a. live
b. lives

CHOOSE

Example:

Where _____ your brother live?

(a.) does
b. do

6. Where _____ they live?

a. do
b. does

7. What language _____ Anna speak?

a. do
b. does

8. What _____ you do every day?

a. do
b. does

9. Where _____ your daughter study?

a. do
b. does

10. What language _____ speak?

a. you do
b. do you

CHOOSE

Example:

He _____ his grandparents every week.

a. visit

(b.) calls

c. speaks

d. talks

11. Maria is from Mexico. She _____ Spanish.

a. talks

b. eats

c. read

d. speaks

12. They're from Seoul. They _____ Korean TV shows.

a. listen

b. watch

c. wash

d. look

13. Every day Miguel _____ Puerto Rican food.

a. reads

b. talks

c. cooks

d. eat

14. We _____ in big department stores.

a. visit

b. shop

c. call

d. sells

15. I _____ Greek radio programs.

a. listen to

b. talk to

c. watch

d. listen

16. My friend Nicole _____ French music.

a. listens

b. listens to

c. talks

d. speaks

17. Mr. and Mrs. Blake _____ Canadian newspapers.

a. visit

b. listen

c. buys

d. read

18. We _____ in a nice neighborhood.

a. call

b. live

c. works

d. do

19. My brother _____ the violin.

a. speaks

b. listens

c. plays

d. reads

20. I _____ in a large supermarket.

a. shop

b. call

c. drive

d. visit

WHICH WORD?

A. | What's   Where's   (Where) | | do   is   does | ²¹ your husband work?

B. He | work   sell   works | ²² in a department store.

A. | Where   What   What's | ²³ does he | does   sells   do | ²⁴ ?

B. He | sell   sells   buy | ²⁵ shoes.

Score: _____

Student's Name _____ I.D. Number _____

Course _____ Teacher _____ Date _____

CHOOSE

Example:

We play volleyball _____.

a. in Saturday
b. Tuesday
c. at Wednesday
(d.) on Monday

1. _____ do you go dancing?

a. Who
b. When
c. What kind
d. When you

2. _____ live in New York?

a. Does she
b. She does
c. Do she
d. She

3. Yes, _____.

a. does she
b. I does
c. she does
d. do we

4. No, _____.

a. don't we
b. they don't
c. I doesn't
d. doesn't he

5. Betty _____ at the bank.

a. works not
b. not works
c. not work
d. doesn't work

6. _____ to a health club on Friday?

a. Does he go
b. Goes he
c. Do he go
d. Does go he

7. When _____ to the store?

a. they go
b. go they
c. do they go
d. we go

8. _____ jog in the park?

a. She
b. Does she
c. Does you
d. She does

9. _____ on Saturday?

a. Do they work
b. Work they
c. Work do they
d. Does they work

10. _____ Italian food?

a. Like you
b. Like you do
c. Do like you
d. Do you like

Student's Name _____ Date _____

WHAT'S THE RESPONSE?

Example:

What kind of books do your children read?

a. They read on Thursday.
b. No, they don't.
c. They read popular books.
d. Because they like to read.

11. Do you and your wife jog in the park?

a. No. We jog in the park.
b. Yes, we do.
c. No. They jog at the beach.
d. Yes, they do

12. Does your nephew play tennis on Friday?

a. No, he doesn't.
b. No. He plays in school.
c. Yes, they do.
d. Yes, he doesn't.

13. Do you and Tim write for the school newspaper?

a. No, they don't.
b. Yes. We don't write for the school newspaper.
c. Yes, he does.
d. No, we don't.

14. What kind of music does she like?

a. Yes, she does.
b. She likes dramas.
c. She likes jazz.
d. No, she doesn't.

15. When does your cousin cook Chinese food?

a. Yes. She cooks Chinese food.
b. She cooks Chinese food on Monday.
c. No, she doesn't.
d. He cooks Chinese food at home.

CHOOSE

Example:

We _____ in the choir.

a. write
b. sing *(circled)*
c. cook
d. go

16. She plays in the _____.

a. tennis
b. volleyball
c. orchestra
d. lesson

17. On Friday they do _____.

a. yoga
b. food
c. concert
d. exercise

18. We watch _____ every Saturday.

a. our instruments
b. to church
c. the radio
d. videos

19. She goes to a karate _____ on Tuesday.

a. lesson
b. sport
c. choir
d. concert

20. He isn't very outgoing. He's _____.

a. busy
b. shy
c. popular
d. home

WHICH WORD?

A. My friend Bob isn't a very outgoing person. He's very | shy *(circled)*   nice   outgoing |.

B. | Does he go   Does he goes   Goes he |²¹ to parties?

A. No, | he don't   doesn't he   he doesn't |²² . He and his wife stay home.

He doesn't | like   go   likes |²³ parties.

B. | Does   Are   Do |²⁴ they watch TV?

A. No, | don't   they don't   don't they |²⁵ . They read.

Score: _____

Student's Name _____	I.D. Number _____
Course _____ Teacher _____	Date _____

WHAT DO THEY HAVE?

Example:

We _____ noisy neighbors.

(a.) have
b. has

1 My sister _____ curly hair.

a. have
b. has

2. My grandparents _____ a motorcycle.

a. have
b. has

3. This building _____ two elevators.

a. have
b. has

4. My children _____ brown hair.

a. have
b. has

5. Does your brother _____ a dog?

a. have
b. has

CHOOSE

Example:

How often does your boyfriend call
_____?

(a.) you
b. your
c. you're

6. How often do you watch TV? I rarely
watch _____.

a. them
b. him
c. it

7. My sister lives in Chicago. I call _____
every weekend.

a. us
b. her
c. him

8. Do you like Mr. Lee? I like _____ very
much.

a. me
b. her
c. him

9. How often do you read magazines?
I read _____ every day.

a. them
b. it
c. you

10. Our grandchildren call _____ very
often.

a. we
b. our
c. us

CHOOSE

Example:

Their son is short and _____.

(a.) heavy
b. tall
c. blue eyes
d. curly hair

11. I don't have long hair. I have _____ hair.

a. straight
b. blond
c. short
d. brown

12. Her daughter doesn't have curly hair. She has _____ hair.

a. brown
b. straight
c. tall
d. short

13. I don't _____ like my father.

a. have
b. be
c. like
d. look

14. Do you jog in the morning or in the _____?

a. evening
b. weekend
c. day
d. year

15. I don't play _____.

a. an elevator
b. the suburbs
c. a musical instrument
d. the escalator

THEY'RE DIFFERENT

Example:

Michael never _____ Italian food, but his parents always _____ it.

a. eat . . . eat
b. eats . . . eat
c. eats . . . eats
d. eat . . . eats

16. We often _____ to Charles, but he never _____ to us.

a. writes . . . writes
b. write . . . write
c. write . . . writes
d. writes . . . write

17. I rarely _____ game shows, but my husband always _____ them.

a. watch . . . watches
b. watch . . . watch
c. watches . . . watches
d. watches . . . watch

18. Jill usually _____ the newspaper in the morning. Her children _____ it at night.

a. read . . . reads
b. reads . . . read
c. read . . . read
d. reads . . . reads

19. Ed _____ his windows very often. His next-door neighbors never _____ them.

a. clean . . . clean
b. clean . . . cleans
c. cleans . . . clean
d. cleans . . . cleans

20. They never _____ about us, but we _____ about them all the time.

a. think . . . think
b. thinks . . . thinks
c. think . . . thinks
d. thinks . . . think

WHICH WORD?

My cousin and I [be   am   (are)] very different. I [live   have   lives] ²¹

in Miami. She [work   lives   has] ²² in New York. [In   At   On] ²³ the weekend

my cousin usually [watch   play   plays] ²⁴ tennis. I [always   usually   never] ²⁵

play tennis. I usually read at home.

Score: _____

Student's Name _____ I.D. Number _____

Course _____ Teacher _____ Date _____

CHOOSE

Example:

Howard is crying. He's _____.

a. cold

(b.) sad

c. thirsty

d. hungry

1. Those men are shouting. They're _____.

a. angry

b. sad

c. outgoing

d. embarrassed

2. He always bites his nails when he's _____.

a. hungry

b. happy

c. nervous

d. tired

3. They're going to Howard's Restaurant because they're _____.

a. embarrassed

b. happy

c. scared

d. hungry

4. I'm going to the doctor because I'm _____.

a. sick

b. shy

c. cold

d. angry

5. Aunt Jane is yawning. She's _____.

a. tall

b. tired

c. thirsty

d. happy

CHOOSE

Example:

She's _____ because she's happy.

(a.) smiling
b. smile
c. smiles

6. I'm _____ the dishes in the bathtub.

a. wash
b. washes
c. washing

7. They always _____ when they're cold.

a. shiver
b. shivering
c. shivers

8. Do you usually _____ your eyes when you're scared?

a. covering
b. cover
c. covers

9. Why are you _____ the carpet?

a. sweeping
b. sweeps
c. sweep

10. When I'm embarrassed, I _____.

a. blushing
b. blushes
c. blush

THAT'S STRANGE!

Example:

My sister is _____ with a flashlight.

a. studies
(b.) studying
c. study

11. The secretary and the custodian are _____ in the office.

a. dances
b. dancing
c. dance

12. Nancy and Bob never _____ the bus.

a. takes
b. taking
c. take

13. Why is Gloria _____ to work today?

a. walk
b. walking
c. walks

14. My grandmother never _____ a computer.

a. uses
b. using
c. use

15. Does your son usually _____ his teeth in the kitchen?

a. brush
b. brushing
c. brushes

WHAT'S THE QUESTION?

Example:

_____ are you crying?

(a.) Why

b. What

c. Do

d. Who

16. _____ are you doing?

a. Why

b. What

c. Do

d. Where

17. _____ the dog always eat in the dining room?

a. Do

b. Where

c. Does

d. Why

18. What _____ Fran and Maria doing?

a. is

b. are

c. does

d. do

19. _____ are their children sleeping in the yard?

a. What

b. Where

c. Who

d. Why

20. Does he usually _____ two sweaters?

a. wear

b. wears

c. be wearing

d. wearing

WHICH WORD?

A. (What)   Why   Where   is Carol doing?

B. She's rides   ride   riding [21] her bicycle to work.

A. That's strange! Does she unusual   usually   usual [22] ride her bicycle to work?

B. No. She always   usually   never [23] ride   rides   riding [24] her bicycle

to work, but she's riding it to work today.

A. Why is she doing that?

B. Because her car is broken   tired   embarrassed [25] .

Score: _____

WHAT'S THE QUESTION?

Example:

    A. _____ he cook?
    B. Yes, he can.
      (a.) Can
      b. Has to
      c. What
      d. What can

1. A. _____ Mr. and Mrs. Kim speak Russian?
    B. No, they can't.
      a. What can
      b. How
      c. Can
      d. But

2. A. Can Fred _____ cars?
    B. Yes, he can.
      a. fixes
      b. fix
      c. fixing
      d. does

3. A. _____ you and Sally skate?
    B. No, we can't.
      a. Does
      b. Do
      c. Are
      d. Can

4. A. _____ job are you looking for?
    B. I'm looking for a job as a secretary.
      a. What kind of
      b. Can the
      c. What kind
      d. Where's the

5. A. What _____ you do?
    B. I can drive a truck.
      a. can't
      b. are
      c. can
      d. can do

CHOOSE

Example:

They _____ do their homework.

a. has to
b. have to *(circled)*

6. I _____ go the doctor.

a. has to
b. have to

7. She _____ wash her clothes.

a. has to
b. have to

8. My friend's children _____ clean their bedroom.

a. has to
b. have to

9. You _____ take inventory on Friday.

a. have to
b. has to

10. You and Herbert _____ work this weekend.

a. has to
b. have to

CAN OR CAN'T?

Example:

My brother is a singer. He _____ sing very well.

a. can *(circled)*
b. can't

11. This food is terrible! The chef in this restaurant _____ cook.

a. can
b. can't

12. Carol is a very good mechanic. She _____ fix cars very well.

a. can
b. can't

13. Michael isn't a good secretary. He _____ use a computer.

a. can
b. can't

14. Emily is a good construction worker. She _____ operate equipment.

a. can
b. can't

15. He can drive a car, but he _____ drive a truck.

a. can
b. can't

CHOOSE

Example:

Albert bakes cakes every day. He's a _____.

a. teacher
b. salesperson
(c.) baker
d. driver

16. Judy and Helen are very athletic. They can play _____.

a. baseball
b. piano
c. cards
d. locks

17. Of course they can. They _____ every day. They're actors.

a. act
b. are
c. acts
d. can

18. Can Bob _____ with us on Saturday?

a. has lunch
b. have lunch
c. having lunch
d. have to have lunch

19. I'm _____. I have to study.

a. skating
b. can't
c. student
d. sorry

20. I'm looking for a job as a construction worker. I can _____.

a. type
b. take inventory
c. build things
d. file

WHICH WORD?

Janet is a very good [(secretary)   superintendent   chef] .

She [can type   is typing   can't type] ²¹ very well, and she can

[fix   operate   file] ²² . She can also [look   use   find] ²³ business software

on the computer. Her husband, Bob, is a very good painter. He can't paint

[customers   house   pictures] ²⁴ , but he [can   doesn't   can't] ²⁵ paint houses.

Score: _____

Student's Name _____ I.D. Number _____

Course _____ Teacher _____ Date _____

WHAT TIME IS IT?

Example:

(a.) It's five o'clock.
b. It's four o'clock.
c. It's five thirty.
d. It's twelve o'clock.

1. a. It's a quarter after seven.
b. It's seven thirty.
c. It's seven thirteen.
d. It's a quarter to eight.

2. a. It's a quarter after one.
b. It's half past twelve.
c. It's twelve fifteen.
d. It's a quarter to twelve.

3. a. It's a quarter after twelve.
b. It's a quarter after eleven.
c. It's a quarter to eleven.
d. It's a quarter to twelve.

4. a. It's half past three.
b. It's half past two.
c. It's two thirteen.
d. It's three thirty.

5. a. It's a quarter to five.
b. It's six forty-five.
c. It's five forty-five.
d. It's a quarter after six.

WHICH WORD DOESN'T BELONG?

Example:

   a. January   b. May   (c.) Monday   d. April

6. a. September   b. Saturday   c. Sunday   d. Thursday

7. a. at once   b. immediately   c. right away   d. next week

8. a. fall   b. night   c. summer   d. winter

9. a. this evening   b. this morning   c. this afternoon   d. this weekend

10. a. tomorrow morning   b. evening   c. tomorrow night   d. tonight

CHOOSE

Example:

Tony _____ his nephews to the zoo.
(a.) wants to take
b. going to take
c. going to take
d. wants take

11. I'm _____ music tonight.
a. going listen to
b. want to listen to
c. going to listen to
d. wanting listen to

12. I think the weather _____ bad this weekend.
a. wants to be
b. is going to be
c. is going to
d. be very

13. We're _____ the beach tomorrow afternoon.
a. going to
b. want to go to
c. going
d. going to go

14. Alan _____ sailing tomorrow morning.
a. going
b. wants to go
c. going to go
d. going to want to go

15. _____ it's going to snow tonight.
a. Says the radio
b. According the newspaper,
c. According the radio,
d. The radio says

WHAT'S THE QUESTION?

Example:

_____ time is it?

a. When

(b.) What

c. What's

16. _____ you tell me the time?

a. Can

b. Do

c. What

17. _____ is he going to cut his hair?

a. Who

b. What

c. When

18. _____ going to do tomorrow?

a. What are they

b. Where are they

c. What they are

19. _____ the forecast?

a. When

b. What's

c. What

20. What time _____ the train leave?

a. do

b. is

c. does

WHICH WORD?

Henry is | being   to be   (going to be) | very busy this weekend. What is he

| want   going   doing |²¹ to do? Tomorrow morning

| he's going   he's going to   he wants |²² to go swimming, but he can't. He has to clean

his apartment. He's | wants   going   going to |²³ to vacuum all his rugs. Then he's

| going to   wants to go to   going to go |²⁴ the supermarket to buy some food. Tomorrow

evening | he wants to see   he's going to   he's going |²⁵ to a movie.

Score: _____

Student's Name _____   I.D. Number _____

Course _____   Teacher _____   Date _____

HOW DO THEY FEEL TODAY?

Example:

Anne has a _____.

  (a.) stomachache
  b. toothache
  c. backache
  d. fever

1. Susie has a _____.
  a. toothache
  b. cough
  c. sore throat
  d. headache

2. Fred has _____.
  a. a cold
  b. a backache
  c. an earache
  d. a toothache

3. Mrs. Lee has a _____.
  a. cough
  b. headache
  c. toothache
  d. fever

4. Mr. Wilson has _____.
  a. an earache
  b. a headache
  c. a toothache
  d. a terrible cold

5. Linda has a _____.
  a. stomachache
  b. sore throat
  c. backache
  d. cough

CHOOSE

Example:

He has a sore throat because he _____ all day.

- (a.) shouted
- b. smiled
- c. shaved
- d. studied

6. Barbara has an earache because she _____ all afternoon.
   - a. cried
   - b. listened to loud music
   - c. planted flowers
   - d. yawned

7. Tom has a bad sore throat because he _____ all day.
   - a. typed
   - b. studied
   - c. sat
   - d. sang

8. We _____ at home all day yesterday.
   - a. sat
   - b. rest
   - c. sit
   - d. clean

9. I _____ for the bus all morning today.
   - a. wait
   - b. rested
   - c. waited
   - d. watch

10. I have a terrible stomachache. I _____ cookies all morning.
    - a. baked
    - b. ate
    - c. bake
    - d. eat

WHAT'S THE RESPONSE?

Example:

How are you?

(a.) Not so good.
b. Mrs. Johnson.
c. So good.
d. I worked all day.

11. What's the matter?

a. I have a headache.
b. I played basketball all day.
c. Yes, please.
d. I feel fine.

12. How do you feel today?

a. I'm glad to hear that.
b. So-so.
c. That's fine
d. I rested all day.

13. What seems to be the problem?

a. Everybody enjoyed the meal.
b. I played the piano.
c. I'm sorry to hear that.
d. I have a fever.

14. Can you come in tomorrow morning?

a. Not so good.
b. I see.
c. Yes. That's fine.
d. Thank you.

15. How did she get it?

a. Her baby cried all night.
b. She has a terrible backache.
c. A headache?
d. She enjoyed the party.

CHOOSE

Example:

We _____ the yard all morning.

a. invited
(b.) cleaned
c. loved
d. washed

16. They _____ the broken fence.

a. fixed
b. worked
c. dusted
d. turned on

17. She _____ her friends to her party.

a. served
b. stayed
c. invited
d. prepared

18. We all _____ cheese and crackers.

a. drank
b. stayed
c. showed
d. ate

19. Everybody _____ about the weather.

a. enjoyed
b. talked
c. arrived
d. waited

20. I _____ a video of my trip to Japan.

a. watch
b. washed
c. showed
d. looked

WHAT'S THE WORD?

| cry | dance | drink | ride | talk | wash |

Example: She ___washed___ her car yesterday.

21. She has a toothache because she _____ lemonade all afternoon.

22. She _____ because she was sad.

23. I _____ to my friends on the telephone all morning.

24. We listened to the music and _____.

25. We _____ our bicycles all morning.

Score: _____

| Student's Name _____ | I.D. Number _____ |
| Course _____ Teacher _____ | Date _____ |

WHAT DID THEY DO?

Example:

Tom didn't buy a car. He _____ a motorcycle.

a. buys
b. buy
c. bought *(circled)*

1. Karen didn't _____ last night.

a. her homework
b. do her homework
c. did her homework

2. My friend and I didn't go skiing yesterday. We _____.

a. go swimming
b. went skiing
c. went swimming

3. Michael didn't write to his uncle. He _____ to his cousin.

a. did write
b. wrote
c. write

4. Bill and Tina usually don't take the bus, but they _____ the bus this morning.

a. took
b. didn't take
c. take

5. Susan _____ to work yesterday.

a. didn't drove
b. didn't drives
c. didn't drive

WHAT'S THE QUESTION?

Example:

_____ your teeth this morning?

(a.) Did you brush

b. Did you brushed

c. Did brush you

d. Brush you

6. _____ to the news last night?

a. Did she listened

b. She listens

c. Did she listen

d. Does she listen

7. _____ a big breakfast this morning?

a. Did they ate

b. Did they eat

c. Did ate they

d. Did eat they

8. _____ to school today?

a. How got you

b. How did you got

c. How you got

d. How did you get

9. _____ a good time at the party?

a. Had they

b. Did they have

c. Did have they

d. Did they had

10. _____ last night?

a. What did you do

b. What did you did

c. What do you did

d. What did you

WHAT'S THE ANSWER?

Example:

Did they get up on time this morning?

(a.) No, they didn't.
b. Yes, we did.
c. Yes, they did.
d. No, we didn't.

11. Did you see a movie last night?

a. Yes, I saw.
b. No, we didn't.
c. No, we didn't see.
d. Yes, you did.

12. Did I make a mistake?

a. No, you didn't.
b. Yes, we did.
c. No, we didn't.
d. Yes, you made.

13. How did he get to school?

a. No, he didn't
b. Yes, he did.
c. He walked.
d. Did he?

14. What did she do yesterday?

a. She reads a book.
b. She readed a book.
c. No, she didn't.
d. She read a book.

15. Why did he get to work late?

a. He missed the train.
b. No, he didn't. He got to work early.
c. Yes, he did. He got to work late.
d. No. He didn't work late.

CHOOSE

Example:

Max missed the _____ today.

(a.) bus
b. car
c. bicycle
d. late

16. I had a _____ this morning.

a. breakfast
b. supermarket
c. work
d. stomachache

17. Nancy had to go to the _____ today.

a. dentist
b. shower
c. bath
d. work

18. Nick forgot his _____ and had to go back home and get it.

a. backache
b. brother
c. backpack
d. letters

19. I left _____ today.

a. my exercises
b. early
c. to work
d. a headache

20. I met an old _____ on the way to class.

a. friend
b. bus
c. car
d. school

WHICH WORD?

Victor (enjoyed)   enjoying   enjoys   his day off today. He usually gets up early, but

today he | gets up   didn't get up   got up |²¹ late, and he | took   did   take |²² a

long bath. He didn't | have   ate   had |²³ much food in his refrigerator, so he

| droved   goes   went |²⁴ to his favorite restaurant and | eat   ate   eated |²⁵

a big breakfast.

Score: _____

Student's Name _____ I.D. Number _____

Course _____ Teacher _____ Date _____

CHOOSE

Example:

I _____ happy yesterday.

(a.) was

b. am

c. were

1. _____ cold yesterday.

a. It was

b. Was it

c. It were

2. Frank and Sally _____ at the movies yesterday evening.

a. was

b. went

c. were

3. Before I bought Wally's Window Cleaner, my windows _____ dirty.

a. was

b. were

c. are

4. Maria _____ on time for her train.

a. was

b. weren't

c. were

5. _____ tired last night?

a. You was

b. You were

c. Were you

WHAT'S THE RESPONSE?

Example:

A. Did Billy finish his milk
   this morning?
B. Yes, he did. _____.

   a. He wasn't thirsty.
   b. He was hungry.
   (c.) He was thirsty.
   d. He wasn't hungry.

6. A. Did Thelma sleep well last
      night?
   B. Yes, she did. _____.

      a. She was cold.
      b. She wasn't tired.
      c. She wasn't cold.
      d. She was tired.

7. A. Was Tommy in school
      yesterday?
   B. No, he wasn't. _____.

      a. He was in school.
      b. He was at home.
      c. He wasn't at home.
      d. He wasn't sick.

8. A. Did you and Helen have a big
      breakfast this morning?
   B. No, we didn't. _____.

      a. We weren't hungry.
      b. She wasn't hungry.
      c. We were hungry.
      d. They weren't hungry.

9. A. Did Mr. Brown wash his car
      yesterday morning?
   B. Yes, he did. _____.

      a. He was dirty.
      b. It wasn't dirty.
      c. It was dirty.
      d. He didn't wash it.

10. A. Did you go to the doctor yesterday
       afternoon?
    B. No, I didn't. _____.

       a. I was sick.
       b. I wasn't sick.
       c. I wasn't late.
       d. I was late.

BEFORE AND AFTER

Example:

Before I took A-1 vitamins, I was always sick. Now I'm _____.

a. tired
b. enormous
(c.) healthy
d. happy

11. Before we ate lunch, we were _____ Now we're full.

a. empty
b. angry
c. noisy
d. hungry

12. Before I cleaned my floor, it was dull. Now it's _____.

a. sick
b. shiny
c. tiny
d. dirty

13. Before Mr. and Mrs. Chen exercised, they were always tired. Now they're _____.

a. energetic
b. empty
c. enormous
d. easy

14. Before Harry bought A-1 Cat Food, his cat was _____. Now it's enormous.

a. tired
b. tiny
c. thirsty
d. sad

15. Before you bought your chair, you were always _____. Now you're comfortable.

a. unfortunately
b. usually
c. uncomfortable
d. inexpensive

WHAT'S THE QUESTION?

Example:

_____ you sleep well last night?

a. Did (circled)
b. Were
c. Was

16. _____ you at the park last weekend?

a. Did
b. Were
c. Was

17. Where _____ your father born?

a. were
b. did
c. was

18. Where _____ you go to school?

a. was
b. did
c. were

19. What _____ Jim and Jane do with their friends?

a. did
b. was
c. were

20. What sports _____ we play?

a. were
b. was
c. did

WHAT'S THE WORD?

did	didn't	was	wasn't	Were	weren't

A. Why _____*did*_____ you leave work early yesterday? _____ **21** you sick?

B. Yes, I _____ **22** very sick. I had a fever and a headache.

A. Did you go home?

B. No, I _____ **23**. I went to the doctor. He gave me some vitamins.

A. Were they expensive?

B. No, they _____ **24**.

A. Was the boss angry?

B. No, she _____ **25**.

Score: _____

| Student's Name _____ | I.D. Number _____ |
| Course _____ | Teacher _____ | Date _____ |

CHOOSE

Example:

A. Was she late?
B. No, she _____. She was on time.

   a. was
   b. didn't
   (c.) wasn't
   d. isn't

1. A. Is your daughter studying?
B. No, she _____.

   a. doesn't
   b. isn't
   c. sleeping
   d. wasn't

2. A. How are you?
B. I _____ a terrible headache.

   a. have
   b. feel
   c. do
   d. am

3. A. Were Tom and Bill at work today?
B. No, they _____.

   a. wasn't
   b. weren't
   c. were
   d. didn't

4. A. What languages does your mother speak?
B. She _____ English and Spanish.

   a. speak
   b. speaking
   c. read
   d. speaks

5. A. When do you see Bob and Julie?
B. I see _____ every day.

   a. them
   b. they're
   c. her
   d. they

6. A. Can you ski?
B. No, _____.

   a. we can
   b. I can
   c. I can't
   d. you can't

7. A. Can you go to the movies with us?
B. I'm sorry. I _____ to work.

   a. can
   b. have
   c. going
   d. can't

8. A. What time is it?
B. It's two _____.

   a. past fifteen
   b. quarter
   c. and fifteen
   d. fifteen

9. A. _____ is the meeting?
B. It's at 10:00.

   a. What
   b. Where
   c. When
   d. What kind

10. A. What's the matter with Timmy and his sister?
B. _____ colds.
   a. He has
   b. They have
   c. She has
   d. They're

11. A. What did you do last night?
B. We _____ cards.
   a. play
   b. did play
   c. played
   d. playing

12. A. What's your _____ name?
B. His name is Walter.
   a. nephew
   b. uncle's
   c. aunt's
   d. niece's

13. A. _____ is he going to the doctor?
B. He's going to the doctor because he's sick.
   a. How
   b. When
   c. Why
   d. Where

14. A. Do your neighbors make a lot of noise?
B. No, they _____.
   a. do
   b. don't
   c. don't make
   d. doesn't

15. A. My father is cooking dinner.
B. That's strange. He _____ cooks dinner.
   a. always
   b. sometimes
   c. usually
   d. never

CHOOSE

Example:

What time _____ the concert begin tonight?
   a. is
   b. going to
   c. does
   d. do

16. Martha usually _____ shopping on Wednesday.
   a. is
   b. goes
   c. does
   d. has

17. Where _____ last night?
   a. do they do
   b. were they went
   c. did they go
   d. went they

18. Is that _____ new car?
   a. Mr. Wilson
   b. of Mr. Wilson
   c. Mr. Wilsons
   d. Mr. Wilson's

19. My daughter _____ a red bicycle.

   a. is

   b. has

   c. ride

   d. have

20. Why are they _____ their apartment today?

   a. clean

   b. vacuum

   c. cleaned

   d. cleaning

21. Bob can _____ soccer today.

   a. playing

   b. play

   c. plays

   d. played

22. Nancy is going to visit me _____.

   a. yesterday

   b. last night

   c. this afternoon

   d. the weekend

23. _____ there a laundromat near here?

   a. Is

   b. Are

   c. Do

   d. Does

24. She isn't _____ the living room.

   a. at

   b. in

   c. to

   d. on

25. When _____ to work?

   a. you go

   b. go you

   c. you do go

   d. do you go

26. She _____ busy now.

   a. isn't

   b. aren't

   c. doesn't

   d. don't be

27. These _____ are heavy.

   a. glass

   b. chair

   c. books

   d. box

28. Before we washed our windows, they _____ dirty.

   a. was

   b. are

   c. can't be

   d. were

29. Betty _____ that book last week.

   a. is reading

   b. reads

   c. read

   d. readed

30. I _____ the test last week.

   a. taked

   b. took

   c. taking

   d. take

31. They don't _____.

   a. want go

   b. want to going

   c. want to go

   d. want going

32. Why _____ you late?

   a. were

   b. went

   c. was

   d. did

33. My son rarely studies, but _____ today.

   a. he's study

   b. he usually studies

   c. he studies

   d. he's studying

34. Susan didn't _____ her hair today.

   a. brushed

   b. brushes

   c. brush

   d. brushes

35. Ted was late because he _____ on time for the train.

   a. wasn't

   b. was

   c. weren't

   d. isn't

36. My sister _____ to fix her sink.

   a. is going

   b. going

   c. can

   d. want

37. What does Frank _____ on Friday?

   a. goes

   b. go

   c. does

   d. do

38. I ate breakfast before I _____ to work.

   a. have

   b. drive

   c. went

   d. go

39. _____ Pamela eat at that restaurant?

   a. Does

   b. Is

   c. When

   d. Where

40. Richard _____ sing, but he can dance.

   a. has to

   b. can't

   c. like to

   d. isn't

Score: _____

WHICH WORD?

I [enjoying   enjoy   (enjoyed)] my day off today. I didn't [get   got   gets] **41**

up early. I made a big breakfast, and I [taked   take   took] **42** a long shower. Then,

my friends and I [went   were   go] **43** to the beach.

Before I went to the beach, I was [happy   enormous   energetic] **44**, but now I'm

tired. Why [was   am   do] **45** I tired? Because we [play   playing   played] **46**

volleyball all afternoon. So now I'm [rest   rested   resting] **47**.

On my day off, I usually go to bed at 11:30 P.M., but I [has   am   have] **48** to go to

work [next week   tomorrow   yesterday] **49**, so I'm [going   want   have] **50** to go

to bed early.

SIDE BY SIDE
Book 1

CHAPTER 1

CHOOSE

1. b	9. b
2. b	10. a
3. a	11. b
4. b	12. b
5. a	13. a
6. a	14. b
7. b	15. a
8. a	

WHAT'S THE NUMBER?

16. b	19. b
17. a	20. c
18. c	

WHAT'S THE WORD?

21. Hi
22. I'm
23. meet
24. Nice
25. you

CHAPTER 2

WHAT IS IT?

1. b	4. c
2. d	5. b
3. a	

WHERE ARE THEY?

6. d	9. b
7. a	10. a
8. c	

WHERE ARE THEY?

11. a	14. a
12. b	15. b
13. a	

CHOOSE

16. c	19. c
17. d	20. b
18. a	

WHAT'S THE WORD?

21. He's
22. We're
23. She's
24. It's
25. You're

CHAPTER 3

WHAT ARE THEY DOING?

1. b	6. d
2. d	7. a
3. a	8. b
4. c	9. d
5. b	10. b

CHOOSE

11. a	14. c
12. c	15. a
13. b	

CHOOSE

16. b	19. b
17. d	20. a
18. c	

WHAT'S THE WORD?

21. are
22. What
23. What's
24. Where's
25. doing

CHAPTER 4

CHOOSE

1. b	6. a
2. c	7. d
3. d	8. b
4. c	9. c
5. b	10. d

WHAT'S THE RESPONSE?

11. c	14. d
12. b	15. a
13. a	

CHOOSE

16. b	19. c
17. b	20. a
18. a	

WHAT'S THE WORD?

21. our
22. her
23. its
24. their
25. your

CHAPTER 5

CHOOSE

1. a	6. a
2. c	7. d
3. d	8. b
4. a	9. c
5. b	10. a

WHAT'S THE RESPONSE?

11. c	14. c
12. a	15. b
13. b	

CHOOSE

16. b	19. a
17. a	20. b
18. c	

WHICH WORD?

21. your sister's
22. I'm not
23. Are
24. Jack's
25. his new car

CHAPTER 6

WHO ARE THEY?

1. c	4. c
2. d	5. b
3. b	

WHO ARE THEY?

6. c	9. d
7. a	10. c
8. b	

WHAT ARE THEY DOING?

11. a	14. c
12. c	15. a
13. b	

WHAT'S THE QUESTION?

16. c	19. c
17. b	20. d
18. d	

WHICH WORD?

21. on
22. in
23. in front of
24. at
25. of

CHAPTER 7

WHERE IS IT?

1. b   4. b
2. a   5. c
3. c

CHOOSE

6. d   9. c
7. c   10. d
8. a

CHOOSE

11. c   14. a
12. a   15. c
13. b

CHOOSE

16. b   19. d
17. c   20. b
18. a

WHAT'S THE WORD?

21. closet
22. mailbox
23. elevator
24. windows
25. cats

CHAPTER 8

CHOOSE

1. a   6. a
2. b   7. c
3. d   8. b
4. b   9. c
5. a   10. d

WHICH WORD DOESN'T BELONG?

11. d   14. a
12. b   15. c
13. c

CHOOSE

16. c   19. b
17. a   20. c
18. c

WHICH WORD?

21. this
22. You're
23. a pair of
24. These are
25. those are

MID-BOOK TEST

CHOOSE

1. a   9. a
2. c   10. c
3. d   11. b
4. b   12. b
5. a   13. a
6. c   14. d
7. d   15. a
8. a

CHOOSE

16. b   29. a
17. a   30. b
18. c   31. c
19. d   32. a
20. b   33. d
21. c   34. b
22. a   35. b
23. b   36. c
24. d   37. d
25. a   38. c
26. b   39. b
27. c   40. a
28. d

WHICH WORD?

41. on
42. there
43. from
44. Jack's
45. next
46. are
47. yard
48. We're
49. My
50. noisy

CHAPTER 9

CHOOSE

1. b   4. a
2. a   5. a
3. b

CHOOSE

6. a   9. b
7. b   10. b
8. a

CHOOSE

11. d   16. b
12. b   17. d
13. c   18. b
14. b   19. c
15. a   20. a

WHICH WORD?

21. does
22. works
23. What
24. do
25. sells

CHAPTER 10

CHOOSE

1. b   6. a
2. a   7. c
3. c   8. b
4. b   9. a
5. d   10. d

WHAT'S THE RESPONSE?

11. b   14. c
12. a   25. b
13. d

CHOOSE

16. c   19. a
17. a   20. b
18. d

WHICH WORD?

21. Does he go
22. he doesn't
23. like
24. Do
25. they don't

CHAPTER 11

WHAT DO THEY HAVE?

1. b   4. a
2. a   5. a
3. b

CHOOSE

6. c   9. a
7. b   10. c
8. c

CHOOSE

11. c   14. a
12. b   15. c
13. d

THEY'RE DIFFERENT

16. c   19. d
17. a   20. a
18. b

WHICH WORD?

21. live
22. lives
23. On
24. plays
25. never

CHAPTER 12

CHOOSE

1. a   4. a
2. c   5. b
3. d

CHOOSE

6. c   9. a
7. a   10. c
8. b

THAT'S STRANGE!

11. b   14. a
12. c   15. a
13. b

WHAT'S THE QUESTION?

16. b   19. d
17. c   20. a
18. b

WHICH WORD?

21. riding
22. usually
23. never
24. rides
25. broken

CHAPTER 13

WHAT'S THE QUESTION?

1. c   4. a
2. b   5. c
3. d

CHOOSE

6. b   9. a
7. a   10. b
8. b

CAN OR CAN'T?

11. b   14. a
12. a   15. b
13. b

CHOOSE

16. a   19. d
17. a   20. c
18. b

WHICH WORD?

21. can type
22. file
23. use
24. pictures
25. can

CHAPTER 14

WHAT TIME IS IT?

1. b   4. b
2. c   5. c
3. d

WHICH WORD DOESN'T BELONG?

6. a   9. d
7. d   10. b
8. b

CHOOSE

11. c   14. b
12. b   15. d
13. a

WHAT'S THE QUESTION?

16. a   19. b
17. c   20. c
18. a

WHICH WORD?

21. going
22. he wants
23. going
24. going to
25. he's going

CHAPTER 15

HOW DO THEY FEEL TODAY?

1. c   4. b
2. a   5. c
3. d

CHOOSE

6. b   9. c
7. d   10. b
8. a

WHAT'S THE RESPONSE?

11. a   14. c
12. b   15. a
13. d

CHOOSE

16. a   19. b
17. c   20. c
18. d

WHAT'S THE WORD?

21. drank
22. cried
23. talked
24. danced
25. rode

CHAPTER 16

WHAT DID THEY DO?

1. b   4. a
2. c   5. c
3. b

WHAT'S THE QUESTION?

6. c   9. c
7. b   10. a
8. d

WHAT'S THE ANSWER?

11. b   14. d
12. a   15. a
13. c

CHOOSE

16. d	19. b
17. a	20. a
18. c	

WHICH WORD?

21. got up
22. took
23. have
24. went
25. ate

CHAPTER 17

CHOOSE

1. a	4. a
2. c	5. c
3. b	

WHAT'S THE RESPONSE?

6. d	9. c
7. b	10. b
8. a	

BEFORE AND AFTER

11. d	14. b
12. b	15. c
13. a	

WHAT'S THE QUESTION?

16. b	19. a
17. c	20. c
18. b	

WHAT'S THE WORD?

21. Were
22. was
23. didn't
24. weren't
25. wasn't

FINAL TEST

CHOOSE

1. b	9. c
2. a	10. b
3. b	11. c
4. d	12. b
5. a	13. c
6. c	14. b
7. b	15. d
8. d	

CHOOSE

16. b	19. b
17. c	20. d
18. d	21. b

22. c	32. a
23. a	33. d
24. b	34. c
25. d	35. a
26. a	36. a
27. c	37. d
28. d	38. c
29. c	39. a
30. b	40. b
31. c	

WHICH WORD?

41. get
42. took
43. went
44. energetic
45. am
46. played
47. resting
48. have
49. tomorrow
50. going

SIDE BY SIDE
Chapter Test Answer Sheet

Student's Name _____   I.D. Number _____

Course _____   Teacher _____   Date _____

1 Ⓐ Ⓑ Ⓒ Ⓓ   11 Ⓐ Ⓑ Ⓒ Ⓓ

2 Ⓐ Ⓑ Ⓒ Ⓓ   12 Ⓐ Ⓑ Ⓒ Ⓓ

3 Ⓐ Ⓑ Ⓒ Ⓓ   13 Ⓐ Ⓑ Ⓒ Ⓓ

4 Ⓐ Ⓑ Ⓒ Ⓓ   14 Ⓐ Ⓑ Ⓒ Ⓓ

5 Ⓐ Ⓑ Ⓒ Ⓓ   15 Ⓐ Ⓑ Ⓒ Ⓓ

6 Ⓐ Ⓑ Ⓒ Ⓓ   16 Ⓐ Ⓑ Ⓒ Ⓓ

7 Ⓐ Ⓑ Ⓒ Ⓓ   17 Ⓐ Ⓑ Ⓒ Ⓓ

8 Ⓐ Ⓑ Ⓒ Ⓓ   18 Ⓐ Ⓑ Ⓒ Ⓓ

9 Ⓐ Ⓑ Ⓒ Ⓓ   19 Ⓐ Ⓑ Ⓒ Ⓓ

10 Ⓐ Ⓑ Ⓒ Ⓓ   20 Ⓐ Ⓑ Ⓒ Ⓓ

21 _____

22 _____

23 _____

24 _____

25 _____

SIDE BY SIDE
Mid-Book & Final Test Answer Sheet

BOOK _____

Check One:
- ☐ MID-BOOK TEST
- ☐ FINAL TEST

Student's Name _____   I.D. Number _____

Course _____   Teacher _____   Date _____

1 Ⓐ Ⓑ Ⓒ Ⓓ   11 Ⓐ Ⓑ Ⓒ Ⓓ   21 Ⓐ Ⓑ Ⓒ Ⓓ   31 Ⓐ Ⓑ Ⓒ Ⓓ

2 Ⓐ Ⓑ Ⓒ Ⓓ   12 Ⓐ Ⓑ Ⓒ Ⓓ   22 Ⓐ Ⓑ Ⓒ Ⓓ   32 Ⓐ Ⓑ Ⓒ Ⓓ

3 Ⓐ Ⓑ Ⓒ Ⓓ   13 Ⓐ Ⓑ Ⓒ Ⓓ   23 Ⓐ Ⓑ Ⓒ Ⓓ   33 Ⓐ Ⓑ Ⓒ Ⓓ

4 Ⓐ Ⓑ Ⓒ Ⓓ   14 Ⓐ Ⓑ Ⓒ Ⓓ   24 Ⓐ Ⓑ Ⓒ Ⓓ   34 Ⓐ Ⓑ Ⓒ Ⓓ

5 Ⓐ Ⓑ Ⓒ Ⓓ   15 Ⓐ Ⓑ Ⓒ Ⓓ   25 Ⓐ Ⓑ Ⓒ Ⓓ   35 Ⓐ Ⓑ Ⓒ Ⓓ

6 Ⓐ Ⓑ Ⓒ Ⓓ   16 Ⓐ Ⓑ Ⓒ Ⓓ   26 Ⓐ Ⓑ Ⓒ Ⓓ   36 Ⓐ Ⓑ Ⓒ Ⓓ

7 Ⓐ Ⓑ Ⓒ Ⓓ   17 Ⓐ Ⓑ Ⓒ Ⓓ   27 Ⓐ Ⓑ Ⓒ Ⓓ   37 Ⓐ Ⓑ Ⓒ Ⓓ

8 Ⓐ Ⓑ Ⓒ Ⓓ   18 Ⓐ Ⓑ Ⓒ Ⓓ   28 Ⓐ Ⓑ Ⓒ Ⓓ   38 Ⓐ Ⓑ Ⓒ Ⓓ

9 Ⓐ Ⓑ Ⓒ Ⓓ   19 Ⓐ Ⓑ Ⓒ Ⓓ   29 Ⓐ Ⓑ Ⓒ Ⓓ   39 Ⓐ Ⓑ Ⓒ Ⓓ

10 Ⓐ Ⓑ Ⓒ Ⓓ   20 Ⓐ Ⓑ Ⓒ Ⓓ   30 Ⓐ Ⓑ Ⓒ Ⓓ   40 Ⓐ Ⓑ Ⓒ Ⓓ

41 _____

42 _____

43 _____

44 _____

45 _____

46 _____

47 _____

48 _____

49 _____

50 _____